BE YOUR BEST

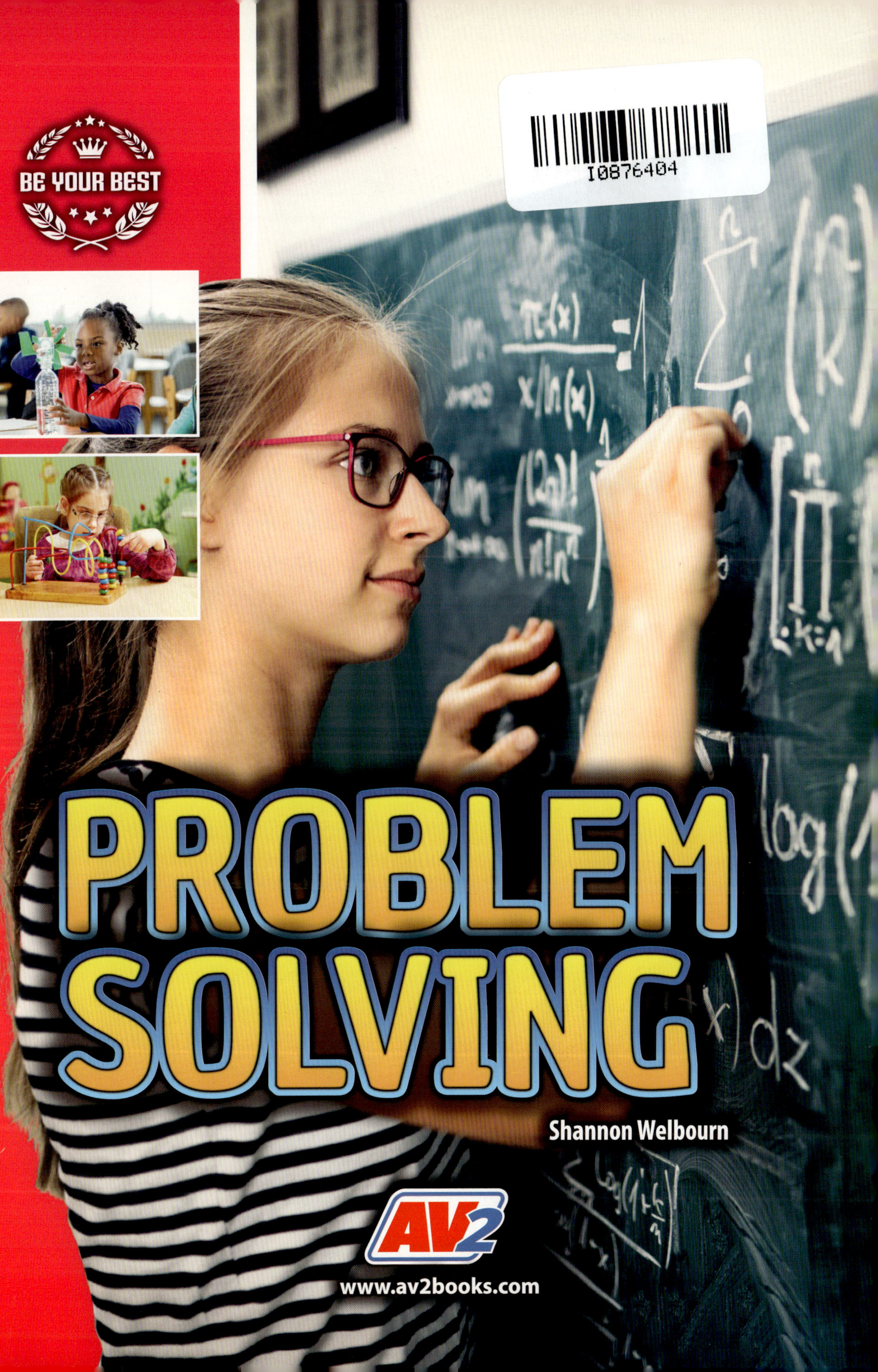

PROBLEM SOLVING

Shannon Welbourn

AV2
www.av2books.com

Step 1
Go to **www.av2books.com**

Step 2
Enter this unique code
WZVYOHNGX

Step 3
Explore your interactive eBook!

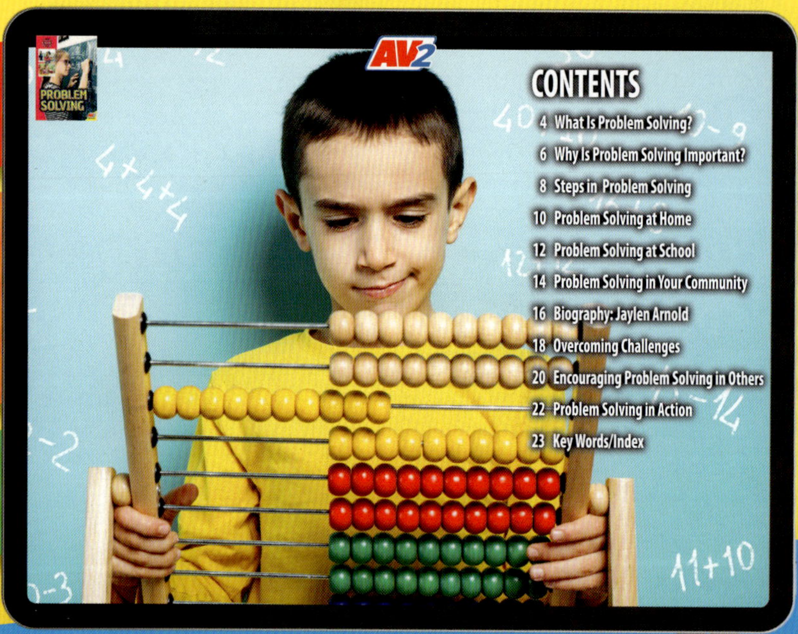

AV2 is optimized for use on any device

Your interactive eBook comes with...

Contents
Browse a live contents page to easily navigate through resources

Audio
Listen to sections of the book read aloud

Videos
Watch informative video clips

Weblinks
Gain additional information for research

Try This!
Complete activities and hands-on experiments

Key Words
Study vocabulary, and complete a matching word activity

Quizzes
Test your knowledge

Slideshows
View images and captions

... and much, much more!

BE YOUR BEST

PROBLEM SOLVING

Contents

What Is Problem Solving?

There are more than 7 billion people in the world. What is one thing we all have in common? We all face problems!

Whether they are old, young, rich, or poor, all people face problems. Problems are obstacles or challenges that get in the way of our **goals** and activities. They may be small, such as a computer game not working, or much bigger, such as getting lost in a new place. When you encounter a problem, you need to find a way around it. That means you need to find a **solution**.

You may also be faced with **conflicts**. A conflict is what happens when two or more people have different points of view on what to do or how to do something. You and some friends might be working on a puzzle when you disagree on where to fit a piece. You think it belongs in the middle of the puzzle, but your friend thinks it should fit at the top. Resolving conflicts tests your problem-solving skills. Finding a solution requires **patience**. It takes skill to solve the problem so that everyone feels satisfied that the solution is fair.

Problem solving is a skill that we gain and get better at over time. We use it every day.

Why Is Problem Solving Important?

Being a good problem solver is an important skill to have. It will help you in many parts of your life.

Everyone faces problems at times in their lives. Sometimes, problems cause **stress**. Arguing with a friend or having a hard time with schoolwork can make people feel worried and upset. Sometimes, problems can cause people to feel unwell and have trouble sleeping. Having good problem-solving skills makes it easier to deal with problems. Being able to solve problems helps us avoid stress.

It can be challenging to resolve a conflict. Finding a solution can take time!

Problem solving helps us feel capable and **resourceful**.

Problem solving can help us resolve problems quickly and avoid getting angry.

Steps in Problem Solving

It can be difficult to tackle a problem. Try these steps to break the problem into small parts and find a solution.

1 Start by figuring out what the problem actually is, so you have a clear understanding of what you need to solve. To help define the problem, think about these questions:

- What do I want?
- What is stopping me from getting what I want?
- How am I feeling? Why do I feel this way?

You and your brother argue over whose turn it is to play on the computer. You think about the problem. You want to play your favorite computer game, and you feel upset.

2

Often, there are several ways to solve the same problem. Think of as many ways as you can to solve the problem. **Brainstorm** ideas by yourself or with others.

You come up with some solutions with your brother, such as splitting up the computer time equally, letting your brother play because he is older, and playing together.

3

Choose the solution that seems like it will work the best. Think about the effects of that solution. Try using these questions to help you:

- How will my solution affect others? Is it fair to them? How will it make them feel?
- Is my solution safe?
- Will my solution create any new problems?

You decide to try playing together. You and your brother agree that this is safe and fair to both of you.

4

Try your solution. After you have tried it, go back and check to see if your solution solved the problem. If it did not help, try a different solution from your list.

After playing one round of the game, you think back to the original problem. Both you and your brother are able to play on the computer. You do not feel upset anymore. Your solution worked!

Problem Solving at Home

Each family is unique and has different needs. There are many ways you can help to solve problems at home.

At home, you work together with your family to solve problems. Maybe many members of your family share a bathroom. This may cause problems when everyone is getting ready for school and work in the morning. You think of some ways that you could help to solve this problem. You arrange a family meeting so everyone can share their ideas to solve the problem. Your father suggests creating a morning schedule. Your sister offers to shower the night before. You suggest waking up earlier to have more time.

Being a good listener is important for solving problems. Everyone should have a chance to talk.

It is important for everyone to be **respectful** and listen to others' ideas. The needs of each member of the family need to be met. Your family decides to follow a morning bathroom schedule. You also decide to wake up 15 minutes earlier each day. This makes sure everyone can use the bathroom every morning.

Problem Solving at School

You spend a lot of time at school. Learning problem-solving skills can help you make school the best place it can be.

You are playing with a friend during recess when you notice that a girl is being picked on by her classmates. You know that bullying is a very serious problem. You also know that serious problems such as bullying are too big to solve on your own.

You should talk to teachers, parents, or other trusted adults about problems that affect the safety or health of you and others.

You decide to ask your teacher for help to solve the problem. It is important to ask someone you trust for help solving problems. Your teacher speaks with the girl, her classmates, and her parents. You and your friend also decide to help solve the problem by standing up against the bullies. Solving this problem takes many solutions put together!

Learn to Make Decisions

Who are some people in your life that you trust to ask for help solving problems?

Problem Solving in Your Community

A community is a group of people who live, work, and play in a place. Your home, school, and neighborhood are part of your community.

All communities have problems that need solutions. People in communities work together to solve problems. Kids like you can get involved in solving problems and making your community a better place to live. Some people may not have enough warm clothing to wear during winter months. You could help collect coats and mittens to **donate**. There may be a lot of litter in your community. You could help solve this problem by taking part in a community clean-up project.

Some communities have outdoor libraries for people to borrow books. You could help create one in your community to help families who cannot afford to buy books. If your community already has one, you could help organize a book drive to donate books to the library.

You are never too young to help solve problems in your community. When people help to solve problems, communities are better places to live.

BIOGRAPHY

Jaylen Arnold

For years, Jaylen Arnold was faced with the problem of bullying at his school. He decided to stand up and solve the problem...for kids everywhere.

Jaylen has different abilities than most kids. He has Tourette syndrome, which means that his body sometimes moves when he does not want it to. He also has

Asperger syndrome and **obsessive-compulsive disorder.** These affect the way he interacts with people. Because he is different, Jaylen was bullied at school. When he was 8 years old, he decided to speak up against bullying. He set a goal that he would spread his anti-bullying message on the internet and television.

Putting a stop to bullying is a huge challenge, but Jaylen did not give up. He asked his family, friends, and other trusted adults for help to spread his message.

NAME: **Jaylen Arnold**
FROM: **Lakeland, Florida**
ACCOMPLISHMENT:
Solved bullying problems at his school and encourages anti-bullying around the world

With help, Jaylen created a website and achieved his goal by launching Jaylen's Challenge, an organization that promotes anti-bullying messages through education and community service. Today, Jaylen speaks to youth around the world on the internet and on television. He believes that if everyone works together, we can solve the problem of bullying!

In 2014, Jaylen was honored with the World of Children award for speaking out against bullying everywhere.

"Kids [at my school] love me for who I am. I want ALL kids to experience the same feeling. I am going to do my best to make that happen!"

—Jaylen Arnold

Scientists believe

1 in 500

people has Asperger syndrome.

Obsessive-compulsive disorder affects about

2.2 million

Americans.

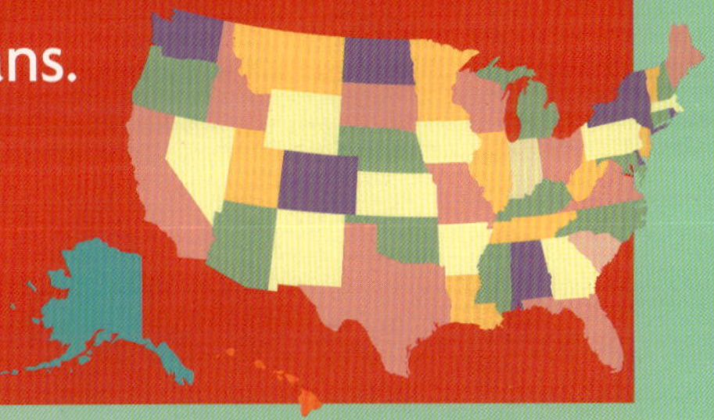

Jaylen has given speeches to more than

200,000

students across the world.

Overcoming Challenges

Sometimes, we might want to ignore a difficult problem rather than try to find a solution.

Most problems do not just go away on their own. Some problems can get bigger if you ignore them. It is important to believe that you can find a solution. Remember these helpful problem-solving tips to get you started.

When you face a problem...

- Think positively. Every problem can be solved with time. Believe in yourself and remember that practicing problem-solving skills is more important than getting it perfect every time.
- Ask yourself if you have ever faced a similar problem in the past. If so, how did you solve it? Could you use a similar solution for your current problem?
- Break down your problem into smaller parts. What are some small steps you can take to move toward a solution?

It is important to try to solve problems on your own, but some problems may be too big to tackle by yourself. Sometimes, finding a solution takes teamwork. Sharing a problem with family or friends can help you feel less stress. They may see your problem from a different point of view or offer suggestions for new solutions.

Learn to Make Decisions

Can you think of a time when you used teamwork to solve a problem?

Encouraging Problem Solving in Others

Once you have practiced your problem-solving skills, you can help others to be good problem solvers, too.

When you or someone you know encounters a problem, encourage others to brainstorm with you. Make sure they feel welcome to share their solutions.. Even if you disagree with a solution, every idea is important, and we all bring a different point of view to the problem. One idea can often grow into many ideas. Finding solutions to problems helps us to feel hopeful that any problem we face can be solved!

Learn to Make Decisions

What ways can you show someone you respect their ideas?

It is important to learn to solve problems by yourself and with other people. Practice your teamwork while you solve problems!

Problem Solving in Action

Everyone faces problems from time to time. Building problem-solving skills can help you feel more capable and free of stress.

Read the example below. Which boy is following the problem-solving steps? You can review the steps on pages 8 and 9.

Nathan and Mika agree to work as partners on a class project. They are almost done, but the boys disagree on the best way to complete the project. Nathan feels upset. He knows he could finish the project if Mika did not disagree with him. Mika suggests they put their ideas together and come up with a way of solving the problem they can both agree on. Instead, Nathan decides to use his own idea without telling Mika. He finishes their project and hands it in to the teacher.

What was the boys' goal?

What was the problem?

Will both boys be happy with the solution?

Which boy followed the problem-solving steps? Explain your thinking.

Key Words

Asperger syndrome: a disorder that affects how the brain works
brainstorm: the act of quickly coming up with and recording ideas without judging them, often done in a group
conflicts: a clash or incompatible difference of ideas, interests, or goals
donate: to make a free gift or contribution toward a cause
goals: the aim which effort is directed toward
obsessive-compulsive disorder: an anxiety disorder that causes people to have repeated thoughts and actions
patience: the ability to endure boredom or frustration
resourceful: describing someone who is able to use different methods to solve problems or achieve goals
respectful: describing someone who is polite and gives appropriate attention to others
solution: the act or process of solving a problem
stress: the body's response to fear, pain, worry, and other situations, causing negative effects to health

Index

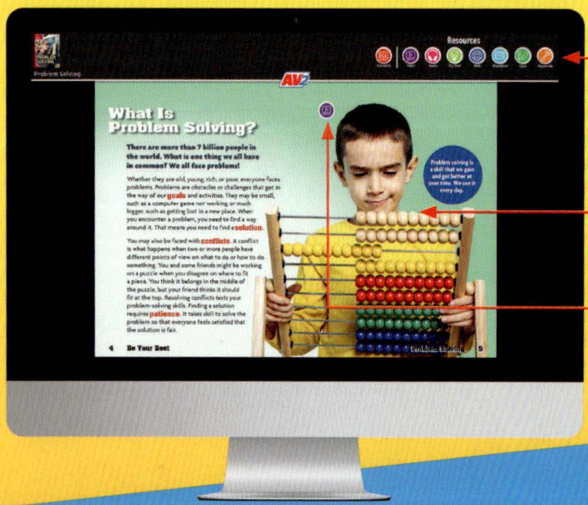

Published by AV2
350 5th Avenue, 59th Floor
New York, NY, 10118
Website: www.av2books.com

Library of Congress Control Number: 2020937049

ISBN 978-1-7911-2791-6 (Hardcover)
ISBN 978-1-7911-2792-3 (Softcover)
ISBN 978-1-7911-2793-0 (Multi-user eBook)
ISBN 978-1-7911-2794-7 (Single-user eBook)

Printed in Guangzhou, China
1 2 3 4 5 6 7 8 9 0 24 23 22 21 20

042020
101119

Project Coordinator: Sara Cucini Designer: Jean Faye Marie Rodriguez

The publisher acknowledges Getty Images, iStock, and Shutterstock as its primary image suppliers for this title.

First published by Crabtree Publishing Company in 2017.